Personal Image Enhancement - Career Edition

Personal Image Enhancement - Career Edition

A HANDBOOK OF 102 IMAGE ENHANCEMENT TIPS FOR EXISTING AND ASPIRING PROFESSIONALS

Best wishes!

Continued Success,

Dwayne A. George

09-DEC-2017

Copyright © 2017 by Dwayne A. George.
All rights reserved, including the right of reproduction in whole or in part in any form.
No part of this book may be reproduced or transmitted by
any means - electronic, mechanical, or otherwise, including photocopying recording, and digital storage, without written permission from the author.

Notice
This publication is designed for reader's attention to matters of
general interest relating to personal image enhancement, careers, and business. No legal or other
relationship is created by publication of this resource. The author of
this publication assumes no liability whatsoever in connection with the use of information contained in this publication.
All information contained herein is provided "as is" without any
warranties of any kind.

ISBN: 1543151582
ISBN 13: 9781543151589
Library of Congress Control Number: 2017902649
CreateSpace Independent Publishing Platform
North Charleston, South Carolina

Contents

With Gratitude ·· xxi

1.0 Introduction ··· 1

    1.1 Welcome! ·· 1

    1.2 Handbook Design, Objectives, Guidelines ················ 1

    1.3 About Dwayne ··· 3

    1.4 Why I Wrote This Book ·································· 4

    1.5 Looking Forward Guidance ······························· 5

2.0 Why Your Image Matters ···································· 6

    2.1 What Is Image? ·· 6

    2.2 Why Consider Enhancing Your Image? ···················· 7

2.3 Appearance Realities ···································· 8

2.4 Behaviour Realities ····································· 9

2.5 Communication Realities································ 10

2.6 Image Enhancement Inhibiters ························ 11

2.7 What Motivates Us to Enhance Our Images? ············ 11

2.8 An Enhanced Image and Your Career -

Imagine the Potential ····································· 13

3.0 Appearance Image Enhancement ···························· 14

3.1 Wardrobe/Attire ······································· 14

Tip #1) You don't have to spend a lot of money

to build and maintain a wardrobe.···················· 15

Tip #2) You can easily mix and match your wardrobe.··· 15

Tip #3) Avoid wearing the same outfit

combination in the same week.······················· 16

Tip #4) Always aim to be comfortable in

your clothes. ······································· 16

Tip #5) Seek an alteration specialist, especially if buying off the rack. 16

Tip #6) Save time; buy wrinkle-free clothing. 17

Tip #7) Complement your base attire with key items. .. 18

Tip #8) Wear colours that make you feel good and don't drown you out. 18

Tip #9) If needed, obtain opinions from people you trust. 18

Tip #10) Don't think your wardrobe is superior to others. 19

Tip #11) Refresh your wardrobe every so often. 19

Tip #12) Enjoy wearing your clothes. 20

3.2 Grooming 20

Tip #13) Shaving - neat and tidy always wins. 20

Tip #14) Makeup - use it to complement your natural features. 21

Tip #15) Hands - avoid dryness and keep nails neat. · · · · 21

Tip #16) Fragrance - use sparingly. · 22

Tip #17) Hair care - ensure your hair is well-kept. · · · · · · · · 22

3.3 Hygiene · 22

Tip #18) Brush and floss daily. · 23

Tip #19) Use a mouthwash. · 23

Tip #20) Consider carrying breath strips,

gum, or mints. · 23

Tip #21) Shower before going to work. · · · · · · · · · · · · · · · · · · 23

Tip #22) Use deodorant or antiperspirant

before going to work. · 24

Tip #23) Wash your hair regularly. · 24

Tip #24) Seek medical advice if you continue

to have hygiene challenges. · 24

Tip #25) Seek opinions from those you trust. · · · · · · · · · · · 24

Tip #26) Enjoy good hygiene and how great it can make you feel. 25

3.4 Facial Care 25

Tip #27) Wash your face at least once a day. 25

Tip #28) Seek a skincare professional if needed. 25

Tip #29) Protect against the sun. 26

Tip #30) Maintain your skin. 26

3.5 Your Smile 26

Tip #31) Your smile can be powerful. 26

Tip #32) Consider teeth whitening if needed. 27

Tip #33) Seek a dental professional if needed. 27

Tip #34) Don't be afraid to smile. 27

3.6 Exercise/Workout 27

Tip #35) Identify what you want to achieve with exercise. 28

Tip #36) Consult a physician to assess if you

have any physical activity concerns. · 28

Tip #37) Try to exercise at least two or three

days a week. · 28

Tip #38) Make a realistic schedule and routine

that you can stick to. · 29

Tip #39) Be patient. · 29

Tip #40) Stay the course. · 29

4.0 Behaviour Image Enhancement · 31

    4.1 Why You Get Hired · 32

    4.2 Understanding Value Proposition · 32

    4.3 How to Increase Your Value Proposition · · · · · · · · · · · · · · · · 34

Tip #41) Understand your organization's mission

statement, goals, and core values, and ensure

most of what you do aligns with them. · · · · · · · · · · · · · · · · 34

Tip #42) Discuss your career aspirations with your manager, and determine together how they can assist in meeting your goals. ···················· 34

Tip #43) Ask your manager for opportunities to do more to increase your capabilities. ··············· 35

Tip #44) Look for opportunities in your office to demonstrate new skills and help your team achieve their individual and group goals. ··············· 36

Tip #45) Learn new skills from corporate learning sources, and look for opportunities to apply them. ····· 36

Tip #46) Demonstrate that you are excited to be part of the team. ································ 37

4.4 Alexander's Probability of Goal Achievement (PoGA) Model ·· 38

Tip #47) High external force goals can be rewarding. ··· 39

Tip #48) PoGA can help predict success. ················ 39

4.5 Continued Learning ······································ 40

Tip #49) Continued learning can be invaluable

to your career development. ··························· 40

Tip #50) Where possible, leverage learning

to fit your schedule. ···································· 41

Tip #51) Course completion certificates and

professional certifications can stand for life. ············ 41

4.6 General Interaction Guidance ···························· 42

Tip #52) Being professional also means treating

others how you would like to be treated. ··············· 42

Tip #53) Deliver a positive experience. ··················· 43

Tip #54) It is in your best interest to continually

try to be respectful and courteous to everyone

you encounter. ·· 43

Tip #55) Have a brand of integrity and credibility. ······· 43

Tip #56) Enjoy your work, and take pride in your deliverables. 44

5.0 Communications Image Enhancement 45

5.1 Email 45

Tip #57) Keep emails concise and on topic (avoid long emails where possible). 46

Tip #58) Avoid embarrassing people in emails, especially if more than one person is included. 46

Tip #59) Use high-priority only when needed. 47

Tip #60) Modify the subject line when needed. 47

Tip #61) Thank people for their responses. 48

5.2 Personal Calls and Web Browsing 48

Tip #62) Keep personal calls to a minimum. 48

Tip #63) Keep personal web browsing to a minimum. .. 49

Tip #64) If using a work phone for personal calls, adhere to your organization's usage policies. 49

5.3 Facilitating Meetings ·································· 49

    Tip #65) Send a meeting agenda in advance, clearly stating meeting objectives or discussion items,·········· 50

    Tip #66) Before the meeting starts, identify who is on the call, and, if needed, have participants introduce themselves.······························· 50

    Tip #67) Be on time.····································· 51

    Tip #68) Acknowledge all participant feedback.········· 51

    Tip #69) Keep the meeting on track by sticking to the agenda. ·· 52

    Tip #70) Thank everyone for attending the meeting. ··· 52

5.4 Meeting Summaries ···································· 53

    Tip #71) Understand the value of distributing meeting summaries.····································· 53

    Tip #72) Meeting summaries should have clear action items and owners.························· 53

Tip #73) Meeting summaries should be distributed and stored in an accessible location for future reference. · · · · 54

Tip #74) Meeting summaries can serve as inputs and background information for subsequent meetings. · · · · · 54

5.5 Presentations · 55

Tip #75) Clearly determine the presentation objectives, and ensure that all content is aligned with those objectives. · 55

Tip #76) Know your content stone cold. · · · · · · · · · · · · · · · 56

Tip #77) Present as if you are having a conversation. · 56

Tip #78) Choose your presentation script option wisely. · 57

Tip #79) Apply a fully-scripted delivery when needed. · · 57

Tip #80) Apply a partially-scripted delivery for less formal events. · 57

Tip #81) Consider using a no-script delivery. ··········· 58

Tip #82) Effectively using presentation slides. ·········· 58

5.6 Social Media Guidelines ································ 58

Tip #83) Avoid updating your social media pages during meetings. ································ 58

Tip #84) Avoid any personal or public posts you don't want the entire world to see. ···················· 59

Tip #85) Employers can review your posts and other things about you online. ······················· 59

Tip #86) Try to keep a clean online image, and recognize the power of your followers. ················ 60

5.7 Résumé Tips ··· 60

Tip #87) Understand that the ultimate objective of your résumé is to get the reader to consider you for an interview. ···································· 61

Tip #88) List all your related skills for that job posting at the beginning of your résumé. 61

Tip #89) Quantify your experience and accomplishments. 61

Tip #90) Don't hesitate to have a lengthy résumé. Vast experience speaks volumes. 62

Tip #91) Never embellish your experiences and accomplishments. 62

Tip #92) Your résumé can be easily reusable. 63

Tip #93) Don't hesitate to have a mentor or other trusted professional review your résumé. 63

5.8 Interview Preparation 63

Tip #94) Practice relating your experience to the job posting. 64

Tip #95) Write down questions. 64

Tip #96) Prepare your clothing the night before. 64

Tip #97) Get a full night's rest. 65

5.9 During the Interview 65

Tip #98) Relax, and get ready to show your stuff. 65

Tip #99) Thank the interviewers for their consideration, and let them know you are excited to be there. 66

Tip #100) Be conversational. 66

Tip #101) Focus on why you are best qualified for the job. 66

Tip #102) Ask questions. 67

6.0 Closing 68

7.0 Log - Image Enhancement Opportunities 69

7.1 Appearance Enhancement - Opportunities 70

7.2 Behaviour Enhancement - Opportunities 75

7.3 Communication Enhancement - Opportunities 80

Dedication

To an incredibly strong and credible woman who embodies faith, hard work, dedication, a firm stance during challenging times, and remarkable persistence to endure all storms that come her way... Doreen George, my Mother. Your influence and example means more to me than you can ever know.

With Gratitude

Thanks be to God Almighty for making this book possible. Also, thanks to my wife Vanessa, and our two beautiful daughters, Jasmine and Jayda. You have enriched my life with your love, presence, insight, and laughter. You continually motivate me to press forward to achieve all that is set out before me and to take on all challenges with faith. For that, I am forever grateful.

Thanks also to my parents, my two brothers Cyril and Wilmot, and my aunt Cecilia for encouraging me to pursue all of my goals without hesitation and with focus, especially toward completing this special project.

Thanks in advance to all who read this handbook and contact me with a line or two about how it has positively affected them. The ultimate goal of this handbook is to be a benefit to readers' career progression and to improve not only their lives but also the lives of those around them.

Finally, I thank all who continually make it a priority to encourage others. Please know that every positive word or gesture you provide is invaluable and can help break barriers. Let's all continue to encourage one another, live with integrity, and Dream Big!

Dwayne George, PMP
BAA, MCPPM, MCBA, CBC, CMM, ICC

1.0 Introduction

1.1 Welcome!

Thanks for your interest in personal image enhancement! If you are an existing or aspiring professional, recent graduate, or student and desire to progress in your career while positively affecting others, you will find great value in embracing this resource. This handbook is about personal image enhancement; specifically, understanding the realities of appearance, behaviour, and communications and how optimizing these elements can benefit your career development and personal satisfaction.

As this handbook is packed with image enhancement insight and practices that you can adopt to assist with your career development, I am sure you can immediately take away many of the numerous elements to complement your path to career success.

1.2 Handbook Design, Objectives, Guidelines

Understanding the concept that your time is a limited resource and that its efficient use is important to you, I have carefully designed this handbook to be both time-efficient and effective. I get to the main points as efficiently as possible by not being too theoretical, while also providing direct techniques that can be easily understood and applied. This should help you with your ongoing image enhancement pursuit. Refer to the table of contents if you need a refresher on topics, and easily find what you are looking for without having to do a lot of reading to grasp the main points and techniques.

The two key objectives of this handbook are to:

1. Have you understand personal image realities and the impact that image enhancement can have on your career, and
2. Help you identify personal image enhancement opportunities, and consider related tips to assist with optimizing your image.

This resource is not focused on technical abilities that are intrinsic to your specific career roles. If you are an architect, for example, knowing the fundamentals of structural design and various measurement techniques are significant technical capabilities you should have. This image enhancement handbook will teach you image enhancement skills to complement your architectural technical capabilities. Likewise, if you are an accountant, this handbook will not help you understand generally accepted accounting practices; rather, it will assist you with image enhancement to hopefully assist you with your career progression.

Now, some important guidelines to ensure you get the most out of this handbook:

1. Take notes. As part of the investment you are making in yourself by reading this book, your continued effort to write down and reflect on things that might work for you is key.
2. Consider or determine what you think might work for you, and try it! A benefit of this handbook is that you can apply many of the tips immediately.
3. Keep referring to this handbook as much as you need to. If you ever need a refresher on any of the topics, just refer back to this book as much as you like. Remember, knowledge does not get "old."
4. Feel free to reach out to me via the contact information at the end of this book. I would love to get your feedback as well as hear how the image enhancement techniques benefited you.
5. Have fun reading this handbook, and be excited, knowing that your personal image enhancement is about to begin!

1.3 About Dwayne

Before we dive into what image enhancement is and how it can assist in your career development, let me tell you a bit about me. Through my academic journey, I found great value in continuing my studies and was able to progress on such paths while building my career. My academic pursuits, combined with career experiences and insights are the foundation of this powerful handbook.

After high school, I attained a business and technology Degree in Administration and Information Management (Ryerson

University). I also obtained a Master's Certificate in Business Analysis (York University - Executive Education), followed by a Certificate in Business Communications (Ryerson University). I then thought it would be best to help facilitate my career progression by obtaining a Certificate in Marketing Management (Ryerson University), and then a Certificate in Image Consulting (George Brown College). Most recently, I obtained a Master's Certificate in Portfolio and Project Management (University of Ontario Institute of Technology).

My studies from various academic institutions were extremely valuable, and I look forward to delivering this handbook based on my experiences and personal insights. Also of note, I have a Project Management Professional designation (Project Management Institute), which complements my present career as the owner of a successful project management consulting firm.

I have approximately twenty years of experience in financial services and government. I have spent the last fifteen years in financial services and have had the opportunity to work with leading financial firms in both business and technical roles. I have gained valuable image enhancement insight through these roles, combined with my experiences, which I look forward to sharing with you.

1.4 Why I Wrote This Book

I have a genuine interest in assisting individuals to continuously be at their best and achieve their goals. There is no better way for me to do this than to offer image enhancement insight and tips that can help people meet their professional aspirations.

1.5 Looking Forward Guidance

This handbook provides various insights that can likely help you. There are no guarantees or warranties. Ultimately, you must decide what to apply to your career or circumstance, and successful results should not be expected every time.

Now, let's get into personal image fundamentals.

2.0 Why Your Image Matters

2.1 What Is Image?

Image is a "general or public perception."[1] In corporate terms, I see this as the relationship between a company's products and services and the association with how the public views the company, its products and services, and the influence it has on the way in which we choose to interact with it. Depending on the type of interaction, consciously or subconsciously, we ask ourselves one or more of the following questions:

1. Should I conduct business with this company?
2. Should I invest in the brand?
3. Is the brand reputable?
4. Will I get value with the purchase?
5. Does the value justify the cost?

Since how we perceive brands influences our interaction, it is a matter of business survival for corporations to invest significant capital

---

[1] "Image," The American Heritage Idioms Dictionary, accessed December 31, 2009, http://dictionary.reference.com/browse/image.

and other resources to maintaining or enhancing their images, primarily for one reason...they realize the significant benefits that an optimized image can yield.

Perceptions exist for individuals too. Individuals can be seen as "personal brands," as when people see us, hear our names, or reflect on us, they associate feelings with our brand - feelings that can influence their willingness to assist us, how they interact with us, and even the amount of respect they have for us.

Personal image relates to how we view ourselves as well as how we want others to view us. Image enhancement focuses on understanding and applying applicable tips or techniques towards optimizing our overall images - that is, our appearance, behaviour, and communications.

In view of the influence that image can have on success, it becomes clear why you should assess your current image and look for opportunities to enhance it.

2.2 Why Consider Enhancing Your Image?

Ralph Waldo Emerson's response is convincing regarding why you should consider enhancing your image. He says, "Who you are speaks so loudly, I can't hear what you say."[2] Let's reflect on this for a moment... As every one of our human characteristics can be linked to an image component (i.e. appearance, behaviour, communications), it is clear from Emerson's comment that our image is important in determining how others view us.

---

2 "Ralph Waldo Emerson Quotations," About.com, accessed December 27, 2009, http://quotations.about.com/od/stillmorefamouspeople/a/RalphWaldoEmer8.htm.

Think of someone you admire, and then reflect on what it is you admire about that person. Perhaps he or she demonstrates one or more of the following traits: courteous, honest, exciting, trustworthy, understanding, sincere, empathetic, or warm. Now take a moment to think of opposing characteristics. Perhaps you have encountered individuals with one or more of the following characteristics: rude, disrespectful, arrogant, conniving, not trustworthy, insensitive, embarrassing, or self-serving.

These conflicting character sets have at least one thing in common. No matter what people who demonstrate these characteristics say (or try to convey to you), how you perceive their positive or negative image influences how you will interact with them. Emerson was correct, and his conclusion acts as a catalyst for image enhancement.

2.3 Appearance Realities

According to Dr. Mehrabian (from UCLA), how others view our personal presentation is based on the following three factors: verbal - what we say (7 percent), vocal - how we sound (38 percent), and visual - how we look (55 percent).[3] Since appearance is a key to how others regard our personal presentation, it is in our best interest to regularly look at our best - especially when we interact with those who contribute to us meeting our goals and career aspirations.

Additionally, clothing and grooming are considered 90 percent of appearance[4] and are, therefore, the most important first

---

3 "Mehrabian's communication research," businessballs, accessed December 27, 2009, http://www.businessballs.com/mehrabiancommunications.htm.

4 K. Brunger, *Image Management, An Introduction*. (2003), 6, George Brown College course workbook.

impression factors. You have likely heard the expression, "Dress for success." This is true for job interviews, important meetings, and presentations where you want to make a notable impact. Dressing for success is not only for periodic occasions - the concept should also be applied to everyday work life.

Let me explain. Dressing for success might imply wearing expensive garments to work every day; however, this is definitely not the case. You can dress for success by being "put-together" every day, which is not difficult to do. Pursuant to an overall "put-together" outer appearance, it can be beneficial for you to have your daily appearance reflect you as a successful person and imply that you are prepared for continued success. As such, I promote dressing for success every day. This is the key to developing and maintaining an enhanced image, since clothing and grooming are considered efficient ways to send messages not only to ourselves (which should instill confidence when fully optimized), but to others as well. Remember that before you say one word, you are assessed by those that receive your appearance message, and your direct behaviour and communications that follow should complement and reinforce the messaging you wish to convey.

2.4 Behaviour Realities

Since our actions can significantly influence our aspired success, behaviour considerations are an important component of personal image management. Would you hire or promote somebody who is constantly negative, does not work well with team members, is constantly late for work, and frequently criticizes team member contributions? Probably not. These behaviours can negatively affect career advancement. By understating the relationship that attitude has on your effectiveness and how those around you react to your behaviour, you can transform your behaviour towards experiencing a more fulfilling career.

The value proposition you offer to your group and organization can also affect your career. Understanding how your capabilities and contributions align to organization objectives can also be beneficial to you. As well, effective goal management can be an enabler to success by choosing your goals wisely.

2.5 Communication Realities

Since what people say, how they say it, and the ability for body language to speak volumes, addressing the many areas of communication certainly helps project a positive image.

Judgments are often made about a person's competence, experience, and trustworthiness just by listening to them speak. Verbal and written communication tools and techniques are designed to align these judgements with what the individual wishes to convey.

Think of a time when you were fully engaged in listening to someone speak, or focused your attention on an important document or correspondence you were reading. You were engaged because the topic was of interest to you and/or the speaker or writer of the communication captured you with the delivery style. Image enhancement helps with message relatedness to the audience as well as appropriate message delivery methods for the occasion to increase the likelihood of successful message delivery.

2.6 Image Enhancement Inhibiters
Unfortunately many people think they are not capable of reaching their image aspirations, so they continue settling for less than what they can achieve. These thoughts are called "inhibitors."

Some of us may have inhibitors from childhood - experiences that have ingrained thoughts of incapability into our lives. Some examples of inhibitors are individuals thinking they are not good enough to achieve particular goals or that the world is working against them. Some also think others must help them achieve their goals, and only the lucky ones get the breaks. Fortunately, inhibitors can be overcome by realizing and adopting tools and techniques to change behaviour, so they transform from being victims to achievers. This often results in the unleashing of a powerful reality called *personal potential*, which is essentially a catalyst for helping them enjoy a renewed life of confidence and accomplishment, as, over time, sustained image enhancement can overwrite previous negative programming.

2.7 What Motivates Us to Enhance Our Images?
Usually something motivates us to move from our current state to a desired state. Whether we want to look more confident, desire a higher paying job, or are looking to climb the corporate ladder, an image consultant provides mechanisms to assist with achieving those goals. By clearly understanding the envisioned need to be met (the "what"), examining the motivation for achieving the need (the "why") can increase the likelihood of applying the most effective image enhancement action.

Now, let's consider the following examples of needs and motivation with typical image enhancement components to meeting the need:

The need (or the "what"): Wanting to be happier at work.
The motivation (or the "why"): Would like to have greater job fulfilment.
Key image components: behaviour, communications.

The need: Wanting to make more money.
The motivation: Would like to provide more for family or to become debt free.
Key image components: appearance, behaviour, communications.

The need: Wanting to be respected in the office.
The motivation: Would like to be more valued by colleagues.
Key image components: behaviour, communications.

The need: Wanting to be better at delivering presentations.
The motivation: Would like to be seen as a promotion candidate.
Key image components: appearance, behaviour, communications.

Image enhancement can be challenging for some people, as it sometimes requires significant change to becoming what is desired. However, when the going gets tough, you can focus on your motivation (the why) for the change. This can help you stay the course.

2.8 An Enhanced Image and Your Career - Imagine the Potential

The following is a portrait of possible outcomes some might achieve (in part or completely), resulting from an optimized image.

Because you recognized a need for personal image enhancement, you read this book, became empowered by potential realization, and understood personal image realities. You adopted and applied tips with a plan to obtain your image goals. - Wow, what an achievement! You can now continually "rise to the occasion" while consistently being at your best. Additionally, you are now more aware of what is required for you to be optimized and can easily access these enablers to continuously feel positive about your career progression and future.

Your colleagues notice the new "professional" in you. You convey confidence, enthusiasm, and focus. You are likely seen as a person with integrity and are respected. You are also more effective and compelling and are regarded as progressive, as your contributions to your work unit have greater value.

Personal image enhancement is a personal commitment that can deliver great benefits, as it can relate to almost every area of your life. Always remember that one of the greatest investments you can make is an investment in yourself.

3.0 Appearance Image Enhancement

As a clean and confident appearance can set you apart, this section provides valuable insight and tips that can enhance your appearance. We'll focus on attire, grooming, and hygiene. We'll then explore facial care benefits, your smile, and we'll conclude with exercise.

3.1 Wardrobe/Attire

Office attire is an interesting and diverse topic, as there are different standards for various careers and industries. For example, if you work in health care, let's say in a hospital or lab, you likely wear scrubs or generally loose-fitting clothing. If you work in a factory, clothing might also follow a uniform standard. If you are a business executive that regularly sees clients or a lawyer, a suit might be your common attire. What this section provides are tips and considerations when dressing for your career.

PERSONAL IMAGE ENHANCEMENT · CAREER EDITION

Tip #1) You don't have to spend a lot of money to build and maintain a wardrobe.

There is a vast number of clothing options available, based on your budget. There are high-end designer brands or labels where optimum quality can be assumed or sought, but fortunately, given the near endless number of clothing suppliers around the world, there are also cost-effective choices that include suitable quality at reasonable prices. Be sure to research clothing stores that meet your budget and quality needs. Maintain a list of go-to retailers that you are satisfied with, and this will reduce the need to continuously wonder where to shop. Also note, with proper care, you can maintain your clothing over time. Be sure to observe the clothing care labels - for example, don't machine wash items that have a dry clean only label.

Tip #2) You can easily mix and match your wardrobe.

To maintain a manageable number of clothing options in your wardrobe, you can easily combine tops and bottoms for new looks. For example, on Monday, you can wear top A and bottom X; on Tuesday, you can wear top B and Bottom Y; on Wednesday, you can wear Top C and bottom Z. Now, on Thursday, you can start to mix and match. You can wear Top A (from Monday) and bottom Y (from Tuesday); and on Friday, you can wear Top B (from Tuesday) and bottom X (from Monday). From this technique, you have not re-worn top C or bottom Z in the same week. Now imagine the combinations you have if you increase the amount of tops and bottoms you have in your wardrobe - the combinations or permutations can be endless!

Tip #3) Avoid wearing the same outfit combination in the same week.
By not wearing the same top and bottom combination in the same week, you will keep your clothing appearance fresh. You risk looking dull and appear "boring" when you repeat the same top and bottom combinations throughout the week in professions where you don't wear a uniform.

Tip #4) Always aim to be comfortable in your clothes.
You should not leave home until you feel comfortable and at your best in your clothes. If you don't, it is likely your confidence for the day will be compromised, as you will frequently feel self-conscious about your appearance. Clothing is an important part of self-image, so ensure that you are comfortable with what you are wearing before you leave home. If you are not comfortable, change your attire!

As you progress with your image enhancement, you should become more comfortable in your clothes. Until you get to that point, give yourself extra time in the morning to ensure that you are comfortable with your wardrobe selection for the day. To save time, select your outfit the night before. If it is the first time you are wearing an item, try it on the day before to ensure your comfort, and to make any required adjustments.

Tip #5) Seek an alteration specialist, especially if buying off the rack.
News for you here - your body type and measurements are unique to you! It would be challenging to find another person with exactly

the same body type and measurements as yours. As such, when buying clothes that are not custom, or tailor-made for you (i.e. when buying from the store off-the-rack), consider having suits, jackets, pants, skirts and dresses altered to your body type or specifications. Getting alterations is not difficult; all you need to do is seek out a reputable specialist to customize your garment for you. Once you try on an item from the rack, and then again after alterations have been made, you should see and feel a clear difference in how the clothing molds to your body.

During the alteration process, let the specialist know how you would like the garment to fit. Your off-the-rack garment might need to be expanded or taken in. During the pinning process, let the specialist know what is comfortable for you, as pinning will mimic the finished alteration fit. Alterations are regularly one-time and cost-effective. You can seek out an alteration specialist in your city by doing an internet search. Also, fortunately many garment cleaners offer this service.

Tip #6) Save time; buy wrinkle-free clothing.

Be particular with your selection of clothing materials. For everyday clothing, if you enjoy a destressed clothing look such as some khaki options, wrinkles are expected. If you are a corporate office employee, excessive wrinkles might be discouraged. These days, it is not too difficult to find clothing that will not wrinkle as much as clothing did in the past. You can look for wrinkle-free fabric options to save you ironing time before you go to work. Heavier cottons tend to wrinkle more after each use, so ensure you reserve enough time to get ready for work by considering which items you might need to steam or iron before putting them on.

Tip #7) Complement your base attire with key items.

It is great to wear clothes that fit you just right and gives you confidence, but what better way to present your personality then by adding complementary items. Kerchiefs, pocket squares, or lapel pins for men can add that extra touch of style. The great thing about these items is that they come in a variety of colours, so you can buy variations to complement your base attire. Similarly, women can complement their base attire with a vast selection of scarves, earrings, necklaces, bracelets, and other distinguishing jewelry options. The rule of thumb here is to not wear an excessive number of these items in the office, yet just enough to give your base outfit that finishing personality touch.

Tip #8) Wear colours that make you feel good and don't drown you out.

You need to wear colours that make you feel good. Depending on your skin tone, not all colours will work for you. One school of thought suggests particular colours for particular seasons, but my thinking is that you wear colours that you feel comfortable with. Try to not wear anything that drowns out your facial and physical features or makes you look dark and dreary, as this can give the impression that you are not a warm and welcoming person. Determine colours that make you feel great and confident, and this can make your clothing shopping more efficient and enjoyable.

Tip #9) If needed, obtain opinions from people you trust.

Family and friends can be great sources of feedback should you be unsure about how a particular item of clothing or outfit looks. Seeking feedback can help you gain perspective from others that you trust and/or admire. Nothing is better than in-person feedback. An alternative for people who are separated from you by distance is to use a smartphone or camera to take pictures or video, and send it to them for their opinion, or video chat (real-time) for their instant feedback.

Tip #10) Don't think your wardrobe is superior to others.

It is great that you are enhancing your wardrobe in pursuit of your appearance goals, but as your confidence increases, be sure to not regard your clothing transformation to be superior to others. Such arrogance can be easily detected, even though you might not be aware of it. The best approach is to remember that you are not greater or better than anybody, so don't look down on those who have not been through an image or clothing enhancement such as yours.

Tip #11) Refresh your wardrobe every so often.

It is great to have a deep wardrobe that caters to the many different events you will be part of - whether it be work, client meetings, a casual or upscale evening out, a weekend getaway , or just spending time around your city. It is best to refresh your wardrobe every so often so that you maintain a "fresh" inventory of clothing options. You will not have to "refresh" your formal clothing options as much as your everyday clothing, as you will likely attend formal functions less often. However, it is good to review the state of your formal options at least one week before an event to assess if any alterations are needed. Your clothes say a lot about you, so be sure to keep your wardrobe current.

Tip #12) Enjoy wearing your clothes.
Your attire is part of your personality. It is also one of the first lasting memories or recall about you when someone initially meets you. Ensuring that you have a tidy, clean clothing regiment is the key to lasting impressions. As you will invest a good amount of money and attention to your clothing, ensure you that you are comfortable with your wardrobe. This also allows you to feel comfortable with your image. Enjoy wearing your clothes!

3.2 Grooming
As grooming relates to the care taken with facial and body hair as well as general appearance, it is an essential part of your personal presentation. The following are essential grooming tips and considerations.

Tip #13) Shaving - neat and tidy always wins.
Men, if your preference is not to have facial hair, ensure that you shave each morning before going to work. Being clean-shaven consistently rather than having untidy facial hair or being in desperate need of grooming shows you care about your appearance, and are well maintained with a "refreshed" look.

If you wear a beard, moustache, or goatee, keep it groomed by trimming each morning before going to work. This shows you care about detail and how your facial hair represents you.

When using razors, ensure that you do not exceed the recommended maximum number days for blade use. Not adhering to this can cause skin irritation. Be sure to review the razor package for maximum usage guidelines or check the product website. For electric shaves, the same applies as for wet blades; ensure replacement of electronic heads or sharpening is done per the manufacturer's guidelines.

Tip #14) Makeup - use it to complement your natural features.

Women, ensure makeup is not excessively applied for day-to-day interactions. Makeup is a key tool in enhancing your natural facial features. If too much is applied, you might present an artificial look. Try to avoid looking artificial in the office if you can avoid it, as it might be seen as distracting to your peers.

Also, consider a consultation with a makeup, beautician, or esthetic care professional. Engaging them will likely cost you money, but they can assist you with makeup suggestions that maximize your features for work, casual, and formal occasions. They will show you what makeup products and techniques can make you look and feel great, as well as how to apply the products. You can then learn to execute their suggestions on your own, in addition to any modifications you make, towards ultimate the goal being your comfort and sustained confidence.

Tip #15) Hands - avoid dryness and keep nails neat.

If you are in a profession where you shake hands regularly (perhaps in a sales or service career) and/or frequently use a keyboard, long nails can risk scratching the hands of others or inhibit efficient typing. As having regular professional manicures can be expensive, investing in a pocket or at home manicure set can keep your fingernails manageable while saving you money. Also, moisturized hands are more appealing and comfortable than dry, cracked skin. Don't hesitate to have a hand moisturizer within your reach, especially after washing your hands, as that is when your hands can lose moisture.

Tip #16) Fragrance - use sparingly.
Fragrance can be a delightful smell, as it can represent a sense of "clean." If you choose to wear fragrance (cologne or perfume) to work, ensure that it is not prohibited, and apply it sparingly. If it is excessively applied, you risk the scent being too overpowering, and prompting complaints from those around you.

Tip #17) Hair care - ensure your hair is well-kept.
Ensure that your hair is well-kept and does not look as if you just rolled out of bed without combing and/or styling it before work. Also, depending on your hairstyle and how quickly your hair grows, ensure that you get your hair cut at regular intervals to consistently present a polished appearance.

3.3 Hygiene
Personal hygiene is extremely important in personal Image enhancement and maintenance. The last thing you want is to push people away from interacting with you because of your need for hygiene improvements. The following are tips for improving and maintaining good hygiene.

Tip #18) Brush and floss daily.

Doing this promotes oral health and can minimize risk of oral disease. Also, it promotes fresh breath, which is required when speaking to clients, prospects, and colleagues. Not much is worse than having a polished appearance, and bad breath.

Tip #19) Use a mouthwash.

In addition to brushing, using mouthwash provides additional germ-killing benefits. Using mouthwash can also increase the likelihood of prolonged fresh breath after brushing.

Tip #20) Consider carrying breath strips, gum, or mints.

This is important when you might need a refresher, or "breath boost" before a speaking engagement. As morning brushing and mouthwash likely will not give you lasting fresh breath to last the entire day, breath strips, gum, mints or breath sprays are additional defenses against bad breath through the day. Brushing after meals is another alternative.

Tip #21) Shower before going to work.

This is one of the key preparatory steps towards your polished daily appearance before leaving your home, as, mentally, it can provide a sense of freshness to you, and help you to be odour-free at work. Daily showering is part of an overall sanitary lifestyle.

Tip #22) Use deodorant or antiperspirant before going to work.

In warm to hot climates and seasons, a good deodorant and antiperspirant can be the key to maintaining a cool presence throughout the day. Sweat can have an odor, so minimize this risk with a good deodorant or antiperspirant. You can likely find a suitable product at your local drugstore.

Tip #23) Wash your hair regularly.

Again, this should be part of your general hygiene program. Washing your hair regularly promotes a clean and healthy scalp and overall hair health. It also prevents unwanted organisms from growing in your hair that can damage follicles, among other health concerns. Be sure to read the labels on shampoos and conditioners to determine a suitable product for you.

Tip #24) Seek medical advice if you continue to have hygiene challenges.

Some hygiene conditions require medication or specific treatments. Be sure to seek the opinion of a medical professional regarding your hygiene if needed.

Tip #25) Seek opinions from those you trust.

If you are unsure about your hygiene, besides seeking the advice of a medical professional, ask an opinion from someone you trust.

Tip #26) Enjoy good hygiene and how great it can make you feel.

Hygiene is an important element of personal Image enhancement, for if you don't practice good hygiene, people *will* notice, and your image *will* suffer. Enjoy good hygiene and how great it can make you feel.

3.4 Facial Care

As your face is one of the first things people look at when they interact with you, it is in your best interest to continually have as best a face as you can. This section provides tips to optimize your facial appearance.

Tip #27) Wash your face at least once a day.

Do this regularly to remove dirt and keep your skin refreshed. Depending on the type of work you do or if you work outdoors or in a warm climate, your face can be a magnet for dirt. To help maintain a radiant face, wash your face regularly. There are many face cleansing products on the market. Try a few to see what works best for you. You can likely find these products at your local drugstore.

Tip #28) Seek a skincare professional if needed.

If you have skin challenges (such as acne) that you feel are holding you back or inhibiting your confidence, don't hesitate to see a dermatologist or other skin professional. These professionals can likely suggest a remedy.

Tip #29) Protect against the sun.
When you are in a warm climate or during summer periods, use a face lotion that protects against long-term exposure to the sun. Not having such protection can potentially harm your skin.

Tip #30) Maintain your skin.
Many products on the market (of which some likely at your local drugstore) can provide relief from dry skin or other skin conditions. I have tried some of these until I discovered which products work best for me. A key cost-savings tip is to ask if samples are available. If so, try the samples to avoid making costly purchases and discovering that the product is not right for you. Also, don't hesitate to internet research face cleansing and maintenance products that might be suitable for you.

3.5 Your Smile
Your smile says so much about you. It is often the feature people remember from their first interaction with you. When you first meet someone, your smile can promote you as a welcoming and warm person in an instant without you saying anything. Thereafter, your conversation can reinforce your appeal. As dental technology and capabilities continue to improve, if you are not satisfied with your smile for any reason, there is help available to give you your best, welcoming smile. The following are tips and considerations towards a healthy, enhanced smile.

Tip #31) Your smile can be powerful.
When you first meet someone, greet them with a warm smile. What an inviting and delightful way to make a first impression. This often

removes any initial barriers to conversation and opens the door for people to be comfortable with you. It can also position you as trustworthy and friendly.

Tip #32) Consider teeth whitening if needed.
This can be performed at a dental office or at home with a dental mold and prescribed whitening agents or whitening supplies purchased at a store or online.

Tip #33) Seek a dental professional if needed.
A dental professional's advice on any corrective action would be beneficial before you attempt it on your own. A goal of corrective dental action is to increase your confidence and effectiveness interacting with others by enhancing your smile.

Tip #34) Don't be afraid to smile.
A smile is a welcoming gesture that makes people feel comfortable around you. Many people don't smile regularly or don't realize the benefits of successful interactions by smiling, which projects a friendly, personal image. Remember, not many people enjoy being around those who are unfriendly.

3.6 Exercise/Workout
Including exercise as part of your regular routine promotes a healthy lifestyle. Most medical professionals recommend exercise to keep you fit, assist with managing your weight, and help keep your heart

healthy, in addition to other health benefits. Additionally, the results of exercise can have social benefits and boost your confidence.

Tip #35) Identify what you want to achieve with exercise.

Whether you want to lose weight, build muscle, and/or tone your body, knowing what you want to get out of exercise is the key to having an effective exercise plan. You can enlist a personal trainer to create a customized program for you and motivate you along your way to a renewed body. If you are interested in saving money, you can use various internet resources and mobile device apps to assist in meeting your fitness goals.

Tip #36) Consult a physician to assess if you have any physical activity concerns.

This is an important point. If you have any concerns before, during, or after a workout program, be sure to consult a physician to assess your ability for exercise and what intensity levels are suitable for you.

Tip #37) Try to exercise at least two or three days a week.

Physical fitness is a great way to help you get and maintain the body you want. It can also be a great stress reliever. Working out regularly makes physical fitness part of your lifestyle. Exercise has tremendous benefits to your health, and whether it is running, weight training, CrossFit, boxing, power lifting, or aerobic classes, you can be sure that your body will reap benefits. On a personal note, I find it to fulfilling to have a hard and focused workout and then shortly after, to feel sore, as that is an indicator of developing results.

Tip #38) Make a realistic schedule and routine that you can stick to.

Don't set unrealistic goals, especially when you are starting an exercise program. You can increase the amount of exercise over time, so don't attempt anything too difficult at the beginning. Doing so can lead to frustration, as you might be unable to meet the challenging goals you set for yourself. For example, I caution against an initial goal of working out five days a week for two hours each session. This is likely too big of a challenge if you have not regularly exercised before. Aim for an initial baseline of two or three days a week for a half hour each session, and then you can gradually increase from there if needed based on your goals and aspirations. If you exceed this in a week, great! Count that as a bonus, but keep your baseline steady until you are ready for your next increase.

Tip #39) Be patient.

Results can take time to become visible, depending on your goals and exercise program. Be sure to keep at it until the initial results come. Once you recognize your process and results over time, that should provide some motivation for staying the course towards meeting your goals.

Tip #40) Stay the course.

If you miss a workout, don't sweat it, just catch up during the week to meet your minimum workout goal for that week. And if you can't make up your missed workout, no problem, it is not the end of the world. Just reset the following week, and get back on track. My rule of thumb is this: if you want it badly enough, you will do what you need to, within reason, to achieve it. Remembering the motivation for your workout program or overall image enhancement will help you maintain your workout schedule when your motivation is low. As boxing legend Muhammad Ali said, "I hated every minute of training, but I said, 'Don't quit. Suffer now and live the rest of your life as a champion.'"[5]

We covered quite a bit in the appearance section, from attire to grooming, hygiene, facial care, your smile, and exercise. Applying some or all of the tips in this section can give you the confidence to assist with your career enhancement.

---

5 "Muhammad Ali Quotes," BrainyQuote, accessed February 02, 2017, https://www.brainyquote.com/quotes/quotes/m/muhammadal148629.html.

4.0 Behaviour Image Enhancement

As detailed in the previous section, how you look is a fundamental image component. In this section, we will focus on the behaviour image enhancement component. Behaviour is very important to overall image enhancement. Whereby appearance can be seen an "outer shell" (i.e. you can physically appear to be component), but your capabilities and integrity are demonstrated through behaviour.

Your behaviour can make or break your development, promotion, and overall career success. Fortunately, it is something that you have great control over. Fundamentally, no one else can "control" how you behave. Others can influence your behaviour for good or bad, but, ultimately, you have the choice in how you approach and react to situations and challenges.

Additionally, effective behaviour builds character and provides an overall sense of accomplishment as you control how you react for the betterment of yourself, your team, your coworkers, and your organization. In this section we will focus on this critical image enhancement pillar, with insights and tips that can assist your behaviour enhancement towards a successful and fulfilling career.

4.1 Why You Get Hired

Fundamentally, you are hired to fulfill a set of needs that an employer has, which cannot be readily met by someone else in the organization. Once you are hired, employment can be seen as a transaction - you perform specific duties, and at the end of the work period, you get compensation.

Your work is largely based on executing "core competencies" (which can also be referred to as technical capabilities or hard skills - i.e. tangible processes) of the job, as well as demonstrating "additional attributes" as part of the job requirements. Examples of core competencies are as follows: if you are painter, you paint; if you are an architect or engineer, you design; if you are an accountant, you accurately present financial information. "Additional attributes" are features you present that cannot be touched, such as demonstrating partnership, accountability, and teamwork. These can also be regarded as "soft skills."

4.2 Understanding Value Proposition

Demonstrating core competencies is not enough to get you ahead in your career as, generally speaking, anybody can learn and demonstrate these skills. What can set you apart are your soft skills - those related to behaviour. You cannot physically touch behaviour (hence it is intangible); however, you can certainly gain enormous benefits by focusing on opportunities to enhance your behaviour "value proposition" to the benefit of your team and the overall organization.

As your value proposition is your overall contribution to the firm, it needs to be clear so that you are seen as an investment that is worth keeping on the payroll or as a promotion candidate. Think of it this way. If you were a business owner or manager with limited financial resources (it is rare to have unlimited financial resources), wouldn't you be interested in maintaining or promoting an employee who not only effectively executes core competencies, but also clearly excels in other areas that ultimately benefits the organization? Perhaps the employee is approachable, friendly and enjoys helping team members succeed. Maybe that person also willingly takes on more tasks and can be called on to assist coworkers or other departments if needed at critical times. Wouldn't this be the profile of an individual you would like to keep on your team and, if possible, line up for advancement?

If you responded yes, you have an understanding of what it is to be a valuable investment to an organization, of who management has a vested interest in keeping happy, to ensure they remain within the organization.

Alternatively, would you value a team member who regularly complains, gossips about coworkers, does not take responsibility, has a questionable reputation, and only does what is needed to get by at work? The answer is no.

Simply put, your value proposition speaks volumes. If your value proposition is high, you will likely be considered an asset whom the organization would like to maintain, keep happy, and possibly promote. If your value proposition is low, you could remain in your position with little opportunity for advancement, or you could ultimately be let go.

So as an employee, how do you increase your value, or stand out? I am happy to let you know that the possibilities are endless.

4.3 How to Increase Your Value Proposition
Here is what you can do to increase your value to your employer.

Tip #41) Understand your organization's mission statement, goals, and core values, and ensure most of what you do aligns with them.
This is important as it demonstrates that you are in sync with corporate objectives. It is difficult for anyone to challenge that you are not doing the right things if you can trace or map your activities and proven successes to most or all of these objectives. This alignment is also important to your periodic performance assessments. Be sure to clearly let your manager know how your accomplishments relate to the key corporate/group objectives.

Tip #42) Discuss your career aspirations with your manager, and determine together how they can assist in meeting your goals.
Many organizations have goals to promote existing employees to higher positions. Your manager is aware of this and likely has a

supporting objective as part of their mandate to foster continued development of employees. To position yourself for such opportunities, ensure that you regularly discuss your progress and career goals with your manager, and ask for assistance in meeting them. Again, this support is often a management responsibility. Explicitly expressing that your manager is a key part of your success can encourage their focus on your goals, while your manager also meets their mentorship and team development objectives.

Tip #43) Ask your manager for opportunities to do more to increase your capabilities.

Showing initiative and clear demonstration of your willingness to increase your capabilities is an attraction to most management, as it shows you as progressive and dependable, especially in challenging times. Do not hesitate to let your manager know that you enjoy performing your job and would like to have opportunities to do more, or learn additional skills.

Let me share how I have experienced this in my career. My first job was with an industry leading, quick-service restaurant chain. I started in food preparation. After performing that role for a while, I was interested in learning how to take orders and use the computer order system while interacting with customers. It was from this experience that I understood the principle of showing initiative and increasing my value proposition, which increased the likelihood of advancement and promotion. As I had the desire to learn something new at work, management allowed me to learn the order management system and order-taking process during low production volume times.

Eventually, during busy times when my food preparation was at sufficient capacity and customer lines were getting long, I would be urgently asked to go up front to assist at the cash registers to assemble or take orders. This provided value to management, as they could call on me to assist during busy hours and reduce customer wait times. As I had the capability to do both food preparation and order-taking, this increased my value proposition. Eventually I got shifts in both roles, and shortly thereafter, I was promoted to staff trainer, and after continued successes, I was promoted to manager.

Tip #44) Look for opportunities in your office to demonstrate new skills and help your team achieve their individual and group goals.

Members of your team know who the key contributors are, and those who only do what they need to, to get by. Once you develop new skills and apply them to your work, it will not take long for others to notice. Don't hesitate to share what you have learned from courses recently taken. As well, try to be available to help members of your team who might ask for your help from time to time. It takes a lot to ask for help, so do what you can to assist them while not compromising your own timelines and commitments. Remember that being a team player who willingly assists other team members is a key component to your value proposition.

Tip #45) Learn new skills from corporate learning sources, and look for opportunities to apply them.

Many organizations offer employees online and classroom training courses as part of their continuous learning programs. One reason organizations promote and finance continuous learning is that they realize that when their employees learn new skills and capabilities, the organization ultimately benefits through new and more effective contributions. It also provides a progressive environment for employees. Attending these courses and expanding your learning can position you as a progressive person, especially if you can apply aspects of the course learning directly or indirectly to your job. This demonstrates that the time and cost investment produced benefits, i.e. return on the investment the organization made in you.

There is always something you can learn. Even if you are a top performer in your role, endless ways remain for you to enhance your capabilities and provide greater value to your organization. Seek opportunities to learn new techniques, concepts, and approaches that can further enhance your skill set and overall visible contributions to your organization.

Tip #46) Demonstrate that you are excited to be part of the team.

Little is better than having an effective and enthusiastic team member. Having good or high energy implies enthusiasm. If you are enthusiastic about your job, others on your team have a good chance to share that energy, enthusiasm, and willingness to continue working with you. People generally enjoy being around people who make them feel good. Try being the type of person who remains calm under pressure, yet continuously offers positive insight to keep the team moving forward.

4.4 Alexander's Probability of Goal Achievement (PoGA) Model

I created the PoGA model quite a number of years ago and am happy to share it with you, as it can greatly assist with your goal planning. You can actually chart the probability, or likelihood, of meeting your goals. Whether your goals are individual or team based, understanding this model can help you regularly meet your career objectives. Let's get into it!

The PoGA model is based on two key components: external force (EF), and personal desire (PD).

EF is the dependency between an individual and any person, group, or system whose direct or indirect involvement influences the achievement of them meeting their goals. Examples of goals with a high EF are: launching a new flagship product for a major organization, bringing a new medical drug to market, having a multimillion-dollar project approved, and securing investment for a ground-breaking innovation. Examples of goals with a low EF are: researching a new product idea, suggesting product enhancements towards greater market acceptance, promoting the need for social causes that can benefit the organization from both financial and reputational perspectives, determining new business opportunities from existing client feedback, and learning new skills to be more effective at your job.

Now let's go to the other determinant in the model, personal desire. PD is an individual's willingness to achieve a goal. It can be further assessed by how determined or committed an individual is to meet a goal.

The following are the results of the model's two-by-two matrix:

If PD = Low and EF = High, PoGA = Low
If PD = Low and EF = Low, PoGA = Low/Medium

If EF = High and PD = High, PoGA = Low
If EF = Low and PD = High, PoGA = High ***Highest Probability Quadrant***

The conclusion of the model is this: if external forces are low and personal desire is high, then PoGA is high. Alternately, as long as external forces (EF) are high, the probability of goal achievement (PoGA) is always low, regardless of personal desire (PD).

Tip #47) High external force goals can be rewarding.

This is not meant to discourage you from pursuing goals where EF is high. On the contrary - you should definitely pursue goals with high EF, if you feel such goals are worthwhile pursuing. However, it is to your advantage to be aware of external forces, as you will need to carefully manage and influence EF, in order for you to have a chance of meeting your goals.

Tip #48) PoGA can help predict success.

The beauty of the PoGA model is that if you apply its conclusion to your goal planning, you can increase the likelihood of continually achieving your goals. Note, the PoGA model not only applies to your current job and career goals, but to your personal endeavours as well.

4.5 Continued Learning

As described earlier in this book, I spent a number of years enhancing my knowledge-based capabilities in the classroom. After obtaining my degree, I felt it best to continue with academics to make me more competitive in my career advancement ambitions. Going back to school, while working a full-time job seemed time consuming, but I tell you, it was the best career development decision I could have made. Obtaining the additional certificates (four from universities, and one from a college), as well as my Project Management Professional certification were both time and money well spent. These academic credentials have greatly assisted me in obtaining job interviews, while giving me the foundation to be seen as credible in my various work environments. My time spent with continuous learning was invaluable to me, and I believe you can obtain similar benefits from continued learning too.

Tip #49) Continued learning can be invaluable to your career development.

Continued learning can greatly increase your value proposition. Whether you have academic or related learning credentials coming into a role (or obtain it during a role), continuous learning will benefit you. You will be positioned to apply the various techniques, methods, and capabilities directly to your role. Given that not everyone participates in continuous learning, you can have a clear advantage, as applying your learning to your role and obtaining positive results is undoubtedly visible, and can set you apart.

Tip #50) Where possible, leverage learning to fit your schedule.

Continuing education can be in the classroom or through online/distance learning. A significant benefit of continued learning is that there is great flexibility in when you take most courses. Many courses offered by employers are online, and you can access the material twenty-four hours a day, seven days a week. So whether you access them during the workday or after hours, the content is there for you to fit into your schedule. Even classroom sessions offer flexibility - you can join virtual classrooms live or access the recordings after the classes have completed, with accompanying content and notes available to you. The less flexible alternative is being physically present in a classroom at the time of the course or lecture.

Tip #51) Course completion certificates and professional certifications can stand for life.

Whether you take a course or program at an academic institution or by a training provider, once you complete the course, your achievement of completion cannot be revoked (in most cases). That means that the accomplishment of completing the course or program can last your entire life. Some professional accreditations such as accounting, and medical designations can be removed if you do not meet the continuous maintenance requirements for the certification, or if you violate a code of conduct requirement.

4.6 General Interaction Guidance

Your behaviour aligns with your core beliefs. Generally speaking, if you value and respect others, you will get the same in return. Remember, you will be measured by how you interact with others, how well you execute your job, and the overall results you deliver. Embody behaviour that is admired, for once you do, you are well on your way to success.

Tip #52) Being professional also means treating others how you would like to be treated.

Be kind and respectful to your team members and all whom you interact with during your career. To paraphrase Maya Angelou, "People may not remember exactly what you said, but they will remember how you made them feel."[6] Whether you are part of a team, manage a team, or lead an organization, the way you make people feel (especially over time) is memorable and can either propel your career or bring it to screeching halt. Let me explain. If people generally enjoy working with you, they will welcome future opportunities to work with you again. That is because you are either effective in what you do (and they relate that to the overall team success), you make the individual or team feel good about themselves, or you notably contribute to the person or team meeting goals. If you are enjoyable to work with, people who have worked with you will gladly let others know. If you are not enjoyable to work with, guess what? People will willingly let others know of the poor experience they had with you.

---

6 "Maya Angelou > Quotes > Quotable Quote," Goodreads Inc., accessed February 02, 2017, http://www.goodreads.com/quotes/663523-at-the-end-of-the-day-people-won-t-remember-what.

Tip #53) Deliver a positive experience.
Similar to trying to give the market a favourable experience with the product or service your organization provides, strive to give others a positive experience when working with you.

Tip #54) It is in your best interest to continually try to be respectful and courteous to everyone you encounter.
You don't know who you will have to work with, or for in the future. Imagine that you had a negative experience with someone, who you may have embarrassed or made feel bad. Then fast-forward, let's say one year later, and there you are, having to work with, or even report to that person. Do you think that person might recall the negative interaction with you? It is very likely!

As we don't know when our paths will cross again with people we interact with, when you are experiencing difficulties with someone, it is best to always consider you might need that person's support or assistance in the future, in order for you to be successful. Observing this reality should influence your behaviour decisions going forward.

Tip #55) Have a brand of integrity and credibility.
Overall, who you are will shine. Based on how you behave at work and interact with others, you will definitely leave a lasting impression. In all that you do, strive to be a person of integrity who adheres to all laws, organizational missions and objectives, and corporate mandates. As long as you do this, you should not have any challenges with anyone extensively questioning your professional integrity.

Also, maintain an elevated professional standard by being a high-performing asset who is known for continuously providing notable contributions and producing effective results. This will surely add to you being regarded as credible.

Tip #56) Enjoy your work, and take pride in your deliverables.

As your career is likely your key source of income, you should highly value your job, and perform as well as you can to maintain it, in order to continue receiving income and provide for your family, yourself, or whatever else your income goes to. You largely decide how effective you can be at your job. For those who want to be high performers, be sure to take pride in your deliverables, as these reflect you.

As you continue to excel in your organization, you will be given high-priority and visible items to work on and deliver. Understand the subject matter and overall deliverables, and be ready to speak with confidence about progress towards overall delivery. An unwavering confidence in your work and team will help with your success. Stand behind your work at all times, as it ultimately represents you.

Your behaviour is intrinsic to who you are as a person and professional. This section provided the reasoning behind why you should be a person of integrity, and how doing so could positively affect your career development. Additionally, value proposition and goal management fundamentals were explained. We also explored the benefits of continued learning and general interaction guidelines.

5.0 Communications Image Enhancement

Business communications take the forms of written, verbal, and nonverbal. As it can be easy for intended messages to get lost in delivery channels, it is important to understand the intricacies of the various delivery mechanisms, as part of your communication options. Additionally, since communicating the wrong message at the wrong time can be detrimental, understanding message execution fundamentals is key.

5.1 Email

In addition to in-person and telephone conversations, email is a frequent and vital communication method for many professionals. In fact, it is common for email to be the most used form of communications in business, as it can be used to efficiently communicate to many people at the same time, and can span multiple countries and time zones to your advantage. This section provides insight on effective email use.

Tip #57) Keep emails concise and on topic (avoid long emails where possible).

Time is precious for both you and your email recipients. Whether you get ten or one hundred emails a day, you likely don't have time to ready unnecessarily long emails. When writing emails, get to the main point of your message quickly. Daily work email correspondence is not intended to be essays or editorials. When sending a message to one or multiple people, be respectful of their time, and keep your emails brief and to the point.

To keep things concise, clearly state what the issue or purpose of the email is, and the requested action from the reader. You can also use bullets as part of your message, as quick points are easy to understand and can help the reader efficiently take in your entire message.

Tip #58) Avoid embarrassing people in emails, especially if more than one person is included.

Remember, given that not everyone thinks or acts like you, challenges and difficulties will arise in your career. When these occur, be sure to have the corporate respect for the other individual. While you might want to vent your frustration to that person or others in an email, you can do so tactfully, without embarrassing or demeaning the individual. Even if someone does this to you, resist the desire to respond with such negativity. Instead, take the higher road and giving a diplomatic response by thanking the individual for the feedback and asking to be contacted directly the next time, rather than through a wide distribution.

Tip #59) Use high-priority only when needed.
You should use normal priority for the majority of your emails. Use high-priority sparingly, as it means an immediate call to action or attention. If you use it regularly, it can lose its effectiveness as recipients may discount the importance of your high-priority items. If a majority of your emails are marked high-priority and you are not in an emergency type role, you likely need to reassess how you use it.

Tip #60) Modify the subject line when needed.
Modifying the subject line in the email header is particularly useful in email threads when requesting particular action or critical response from an individual or group. It is effective as it grabs attention. Let me explain. When you send an email and it appears in a recipient's preview inbox, it is not always immediately clear if the email was sent to you directly for a response or to others as well, and you need to open it to know for sure. Amending the beginning of the subject line with your call to action, such as, "Direction from Ralph needed..." (followed by the existing subject line), grabs attention and lets Ralph know he needs to respond quickly. As Ralph receives a large number of emails per day, identifying him in the subject line is likely to get his attention for a timely response.

Depending on your organization or group, modifying the subject line might not be encouraged, as maintaining entire email threads by subject line sort is needed for analytics or issue tracking purposes. Check with your manager or organization to determine if any such restrictions are in place.

Tip #61) Thank people for their responses.

In the beginning of my response to someone, I like to thank the person who sent me the email. I do this for approximately 95 percent of my initial email responses. Whether the email is a request for information, an issue tracking item, a bad news email, or just regular correspondence, thanking the person for writing you directly or including you on a group distribution shows you appreciate receiving the email and the time taken to create it. It also readies the individual for your response. Whether your response is favourable or not, the initial thanks should generally make the receiver feel good about you, and attract attention for your response. It also shows you as courteous and respectful. Remember, people generally enjoy interacting with courteous and respectful people.

5.2 Personal Calls and Web Browsing

Obviously, during the course of your work-week, you will have the need to engage in personal items related to you, your family, and friends. This section provides general guidance to managing these personal interactions.

Tip #62) Keep personal calls to a minimum.

You are likely to get personal calls at work on either your desk phone or cell phone. Where possible, keep such calls at a minimum, or try to have these conversations away from your desk, like in a vacant meeting room. If privacy is important to you, taking such personal calls away from your desk ensures that those around you cannot hear private details. Also, it encourages a professional environment, for you are expected to be tending to work items when you are at work. Your colleagues are not interested in hearing your telephone conversation regarding your payment arrangements for a cable bill or planning details for your spouse's upcoming birthday.

Tip #63) Keep personal web browsing to a minimum.
Given that many office spaces today are open concept, it is likely that people pass your desk regularly. If so, they can see details on your computer or cell phone when you are using them. As some people take interest in looking at your computer screen or cell phone when you are browsing or typing, utilize a privacy screen if needed, or complete personal browsing away from your desk in a private area (if it is permitted at your organization).

Tip #64) If using a work phone for personal calls, adhere to your organization's usage policies.
Whether your organization provides you with a desk phone and/or cell phone, be sure to adhere to your organization's usage polices. Your device usage can likely be tracked. Don't use either of these phones for extended personal matters, including personal long-distance calling. Since these calls can incur long-distance billing charges, they can easily be traced back to your phone. Not adhering to your organization's polices in this regard can not only lead to an embarrassing email or conversation with your manager, but could also result in revoking of phone privileges or even employment termination.

5.3 Facilitating Meetings
Conducting meetings (especially on challenging topics with various personalities), is not always easy. As it is very likely you will have to

lead meetings during your career, the following tips are designed to assist you in successfully facilitating meetings.

Tip #65) Send a meeting agenda in advance, clearly stating meeting objectives or discussion items,

This is a staple to any meeting invitation. As time spent during a workday is important to most, it should be clear why the meeting is needed. Having a set of objectives or discussion items answers the questions to the invite recipients of why they are needed at the meeting, and what is being covered.

Sending these important details in advance also gives participants the opportunity to prepare initial thoughts for the meeting or obtain any necessary background material in order to effectively contribute to the discussion. Also, if participants are unable to attend the meeting, based on the agenda, they can request a replacement to join for them.

Tip #66) Before the meeting starts, identify who is on the call, and, if needed, have participants introduce themselves.

It is important for everyone to know who has joined a meeting before it starts. Whether it be a face-to-face meeting (with a conference call for those unable to join in-person) or just a conference call, identify all people present at a meeting, as those on the phone will not know who is in on the line. To do this, before you start your meeting, simply ask everyone to identify themselves. You might want to preface this by saying no more than names and the units they work for, to keep introductions brief so the meeting can move on. Be sure to write down their names (as you will likely need to refer to the list later in the meeting) to remember who is present. Also, identifying the participants on the phone as well as those in the room will let everyone know who is present.

Tip #67) Be on time.

As you are the meeting organizer, be on time to start the meeting at the time you stated. Remember, as time is precious during the workday, those accepting your meeting sees it as worth their time to attend, so having them waiting for you to open the meeting is not an effective use of their time.

Whether you are going to be five or ten minutes late for any reason, notify all participants, and let them know the modified start time. As a courtesy, keep the ending time the same as initially stated, as to not to further inconvenience meeting participants if they already have commitments following the original meeting end time.

Tip #68) Acknowledge all participant feedback.

Whether the meeting is an informative session or a brainstorming format, acknowledge all feedback, and do not dismiss any ideas or contributions. Dismissing participant feedback can make individuals feel like not contributing to the session any more, and you can miss something valuable they have to say. Not all participant feedback can be constructive to the meeting objective, and if any such feedback received, you can simply note that it is a good point and will be considered with all other items.

The key point is that everyone invited to participate in a meeting is expected to add some type of value, and as a meeting chairperson or facilitator, it is your job to keep the participants engaged, with open communication throughout the meeting. Not accepting feedback at a meeting can close important communication channels.

Tip #69) Keep the meeting on track by sticking to the agenda.

It can be easy for meetings to get off track. As the meeting chairperson, a key duty you have is keeping discussions focused on the agenda items, in order to achieve your overall meeting objectives within the allotted meeting time. If someone deviates from the discussion, there is nothing wrong with you interrupting, thanking the participant for the insight, and then bringing focus back to the meeting. Again, you must encourage contributions to the meeting from all attendees and avoid making them feel silly for asking questions you think they should not have asked. This will likely not only keep them from participating for the balance of the meeting, but perhaps others as well as they may think you will not value their contributions either, and make them feel undervalued too.

Tip #70) Thank everyone for attending the meeting.

In order to bring closure to your meeting, recap the notable items for follow-up (action items), and let participants know if you will be sending out a summary. Finally, as a courtesy to all who joined your meeting, thank them for coming. Doing this shows your appreciation for them attending, and lets them know their contributions are valued.

5.4 Meeting Summaries

I cannot emphasize enough the importance of creating and distributing meeting summaries after important meetings have concluded. As meeting summaries are the "book of record" for the session, it is important for you to consider the following tips.

Tip #71) Understand the value of distributing meeting summaries.

Especially for important meetings where significant outcomes are achieved and notable actions identified, it is imperative to send out meeting summaries. Meeting summaries are important, as they serve as the "book of record" of discussion items, decisions, and actions from the gatherings. As time passes, it is common for meeting summaries to be referred to, as key items can be forgotten. Also, for those who did not attend a meeting, they serve as recaps.

Typically, it is not efficient to document word-for-word what people say in meetings (this is what digital recordings are for). A guiding principle on what to include in a meeting summary is this: if forgetting or misinterpreting a discussed item (or action) can have negative implications or risks, include it in the meeting summary.

Tip #72) Meeting summaries should have clear action items and owners.

Where follow-up items are determined throughout the meeting, these action items should be clearly understood by the person responsible for completing the action. Also, the actions should have target completion dates. Having action items in the meeting summaries serves as a catalogue of agreed follow-up items from the meeting and can serve as status update items for subsequent meetings. Another good practice is to send periodic updates to stakeholders on the status of the action items - specifically, whether the item is still open or complete and, if still open, the latest update on the action's progress to it eventually being completed, or closed.

Tip #73) Meeting summaries should be distributed and stored in an accessible location for future reference.

As a meeting summary is the "book of record" for meetings, it should be distributed to the participants and stakeholders shortly after the meeting and stored on an accessible repository for easy access for those who might need it in the future. You will need to ensure that the location where it is being stored meets the required security classification and/or ensure that applicable security features are part of the document. Be sure to consult with your manager or organization for any security requirements you will need to follow.

Tip #74) Meeting summaries can serve as inputs and background information for subsequent meetings.

Meeting summaries provide great background information for future meetings. If you have a follow-up meeting to continue discussion or update action items, send your meeting participants the previous meeting summary as a reference. This will help frame your meeting early to participants and let them know the focus items, especially, any actions they might have been assigned and will need to provide updates on.

5.5 Presentations

Since you will likely give presentations on various topics through your career, whether at a small meeting, for a large audience in an auditorium, or online, it is important for you to understand various presentation realities and fundamentals to effective deliveries.

Tip #75) Clearly determine the presentation objectives, and ensure that all content is aligned with those objectives.

Whether you are delivering an informative, training, or call-to-action presentation, you must have a clear idea why you are presenting and what you want to convey to your audience. For example, let's say you are delivering a presentation on the importance of fundraising. You might be presenting to give awareness on:

1. Why community fundraising is necessary for an organization, and
2. Where the funds will go.

To further support and personalize these two points, what you want to convey to your audience can be:

1. Why they should contribute their time and/or monetary contribution to the effort, and
2. Why they too should be a champion for the efforts, with emphasis on promoting it to others.

Once you can answer why you are presenting and what you want to convey (i.e. your objectives), you have the cornerstone towards creating a presentation blueprint. The presentation content thereafter will need to align with or support your stated objectives. Think of your objectives as the key direction or focus of your presentation. At the end of the presentation, your key goal should be to ensure that your presentation objectives have been clearly delivered, and fulfilled by your supporting material.

Tip #76) Know your content stone cold.

This is an important point. Whether your delivery is scripted or not, truly knowing your material can give you confidence as you deliver it, and you will engage your audience with a conversational tone. Additionally, preparation and knowing your material can allow you to be more relaxed than if you were unprepared. Note: if you are not as prepared as you should be, your audience will likely tell, as your delivery will be less effective than if you were prepared and truly knew your content.

Tip #77) Present as if you are having a conversation.

For the most part, no one enjoys listening to a "robot" present, as the tone is much the same through the entire presentation, with no audience engagement or feeling. In order to keep your audience interested (other than through the content), engage them by being conversational - make eye contact, ensure you vary your tone, take pauses, and don't rush through your material. Ideally, present as if you were having a conversation with your audience, with the exception that they will not respond verbally but will with nonverbal actions, such as eye contact and head gestures.

Tip #78) Choose your presentation script option wisely.

Ultimately, you will need to decide which scripted option to use (fully scripted, partially scripted, or no-script). My rule of thumb is, depending on the occasion, and how significant an outcome can be if you forget to say something, or if you are likely to miss an important point to fulfilling your presentation objective, you should use a fully or partially scripted (point form) delivery. Otherwise, you can adopt a no-script format.

Tip #79) Apply a fully-scripted delivery when needed.

A key purpose of a fully-scripted delivery is to logically progress through a series of well-connected thoughts, and eventually come to a meaningful conclusion. You should have three main components to a scripted delivery: an introduction, body, and conclusion. It is scripted because the points you want to make are important, they need to be delivered in a particular sequence, and there is content you cannot risk forgetting. When preparing your script, you will likely have numerous updates or versions before you are satisfied with the final product.

Tip #80) Apply a partially-scripted delivery for less formal events.

For less formal and less structured events, a partially-scripted delivery can be used. Include the key points you want to make on the script, and use them as a launch pad for your verbal content delivery. As not all of your content will be read from your script, you have the opportunity to connect more with your audience with eye contact. As such, make eye contact with every part of the room as you execute your delivery to ensure a conversation-like delivery.

Tip #81) Consider using a no-script delivery.
For less formal and less structured events, where a scripted delivery is not used, you can consider using no-script. Usually these deliveries are relatively short and have minimal risk of you forgetting key points towards achieving your presentation objectives. As there is no-script to divert your attention, you have the opportunity for maximum connection with your audience. Make eye contact with your audience to engage them as you present to them.

Tip #82) Effectively using presentation slides.
Whether your presentation is scripted or not, you have the opportunity to use presentation slides that provide visuals (text, images, videos) to your audience on a large screen. If you choose to use slides, keep content to a minimum on each slide, and ensure to list just your key points. Also, don't overuse bold or underline formatting for emphasis, as it can lose its effectiveness.

5.6 Social Media Guidelines
It is likely that you or someone you know has at least one social media account. As social media is a common communication channel used daily by millions around the world, it is imperative that you manage your use of it as best you can. The following tips can assist with effective social media use, related to your image.

Tip #83) Avoid updating your social media pages during meetings.
As many social media posts contain the date and time that you posted something, do not post items during meetings. It is possible

that those who were at the meeting (or were aware of it taking place) who are also connected with you on social media can recognize that you were posting when your full attention should have been on the meeting. A rule of thumb here is to avoid posting items during your workday, where possible.

Tip #84) Avoid any personal or public posts you don't want the entire world to see.

Realize that anything you post on social media can become visible to the world - even personal posts. This includes messages and pictures. Even if you delete something, it is possible that a copy has already been stored on a server or that someone has already captured the screen content. The rule of thumb is, if you don't want a post accessible to the world, don't post it in the first place.

Tip #85) Employers can review your posts and other things about you online.

As pretty much anything about you can be posted on the Internet, this can include you in less-than-flattering messages or photo moments. As you cannot entirely prevent people posting these unfortunate instances of you, you need to be aware of this reality. As such, try your best to avoid such captures in the first place. As employers have access to social media and can easily "research you" on the web to determine if you might be a brand liability to them (i.e. if any significant concerns present about you that can harm their corporate brand or image if they hire you). They have no desire to hire someone who might hurt their corporate brand. You can regret such unflattering posts all you want, but the reality is, not only can it be difficult to have them deleted, but it can also be difficult to prevent employers from seeing them, especially if the posts are public.

Tip #86) Try to keep a clean online image, and recognize the power of your followers.

Although you cannot entirely prevent people from writing negative things about you, try to keep as clean an online image as you can. You can do this by posting as many encouraging posts as possible, so that your followers regard you in a positive light. If you constantly write negative messages in your posts, you should not be surprised about the numerous negative response posts you might receive.

It is important to understand that your social media followers can be advocates for you when negative posts present themselves against you. You might be pleasantly surprised and indebted to any one of your followers who responds in your defense, to less flattering things said about you on social media sites.

5.7 Résumé Tips

It is beneficial for professionals to not only have a résumé, but to ensure it is kept up-to-date, even if not seeking another position at that time. You never know when an opportunity will arise where a resume is needed, and if one does, you don't want to be scrambling to update your résumé in order to meet a submission deadline.

Tip #87) Understand that the ultimate objective of your résumé is to get the reader to consider you for an interview.

For most job openings, there are many candidates for whom a recruiter or hiring manager must quickly review résumés to narrow down a list of candidates for interviews. As your objective is to get an interview, you need to understand that your résumé needs to stand out from the rest of your competition. As such, you need to try to be in the reader's shoes, and ask, why should I request an interview with this person? Having a reader mindset will help you understand how to best present your credentials in your résumé, and ultimately have the reader want to contact you. The tips in this section can help you stand out and increase your likelihood of getting interviews.

Tip #88) List all your related skills for that job posting at the beginning of your résumé.

As reader attention is typically captured at the beginning of your résumé, you need to grab their interest early, so they'll want to read your entire résumé. To help do this, use a section called "Highlights of Related Experience" to briefly outline your capabilities and career accomplishments that are directly related to the job posting to which you are applying. This way, the recruiter or manager can see upfront that you are qualified for the position and can be motivated to continue reading your résumé.

Tip #89) Quantify your experience and accomplishments.

It is great to say that you managed many projects, contributed greatly to sales, empowered several employees, and have consistently been part of charitable initiatives, but without numbers or statistics to make these claims real or relevant, they will lose their true meaning. Wherever possible, quantify your experience and accomplishments. Note: numbers speak volumes and provide firm and real context.

Tip #90) Don't hesitate to have a lengthy résumé. Vast experience speaks volumes.

There is nothing wrong with having a lengthy résumé. Don't constrain yourself with a predetermined page count. More is better than less in this regard. If you have extensive experience, have your résumé show that. Recruiters or managers can become impressed with comprehensive and solid experience, so don't hesitate to model this on your résumé. It can help you get an interview. An example of this is a younger person coming out of school. In most cases, such entrants to the workforce are encouraged to build up experience, and, over time, they can qualify for senior roles. As they progress in their career, their experience also increases, and so too should their résumé content evolve over time.

Tip #91) Never embellish your experiences and accomplishments.

This tip should go without saying. Never embellish or overstate your experiences and accomplishments on your résumé. If the potential employer looks to verify your claims (before or after an interview) and learns of embellishments or falsehoods, it is possible the organization will put your name on a "do not contact" list. Additionally, if you are hired and it is discovered later that you were not truthful with your background, the employer might have legal grounds to dismiss you. Would you hire someone who lies on their résumé? - Likely not. Embellishing or overstating your background can have devastating image consequences, so it is best to always avoid this.

Tip #92) Your résumé can be easily reusable.
As I mentioned earlier about the résumé section called "Highlights of Related Experience," you can customize this section for each job you are applying for, and, for the most part, leave the rest of your résumé untouched. This makes your résumé reusable, with customization primarily needed for that one section. This can save you time, yet have your résumé both effective and relevant for the job you are applying for.

Tip #93) Don't hesitate to have a mentor or other trusted professional review your résumé.
Your résumé is a valuable document that represents your capabilities and is used as a tool to get you an interview. Given the importance of this document, it is recommended to have a mentor or someone you trust review it. As you might not catch some spelling or grammatical items for correction, it is always a good idea to have another set of eyes perform such a review. Also, the person you ask to review your résumé might suggest other areas for improvement.

5.8 Interview Preparation
Securing an interview is a big deal. It shows you have the interest of the hiring organization, and they are willing to invest their time in getting to know you better to further assess you for the available

opportunity. Before any interview, it is best to prepare. This section provides interview preparation tips.

Tip #94) Practice relating your experience to the job posting.

The reason you are invited to an interview is that, through your résumé, you demonstrated the potential to be an ideal candidate for the role. Now that you have passed the résumé hurdle, as part of your interview preparation focus on discussing your previous experience and how it relates to the job posting in greater detail. It is likely the interview will be in a question-and-answer format, so ensure that you are familiar with the job posting content and your related experience.

Tip #95) Write down questions.

You will most certainly have questions about the job you are applying for. Typical questions include hours of work, opportunity for overtime, training and continued learning opportunities, dynamics of stakeholders, opportunities for career growth. You will also have other specific questions about the job. Write these questions down, as you will need to ask them sometime in the interview. The responses you receive will confirm for you if you are further interested in the job.

Tip #96) Prepare your clothing the night before.

To avoid rushing on the day of the interview, do as much preparation as possible the day before. This includes ensuring your clothing is clean, pressed (if needed), and ready to put on, shoes shined, and all other appearance essentials are in order. Getting this preparation completed the day before can help you avoid being delayed the day of the interview, as aside from a catastrophe, being late to an interview is never acceptable.

Tip #97) Get a full night's rest.
As a job interview is a big deal, ensure you are well-rested for this important meeting. Whether your interview is in the morning or afternoon, get a good night's sleep the night before. Get to bed early so that you are refreshed the day of the interview. You certainly do not want to look tired at the interview, so give yourself all the rest you need.

5.9 During the Interview
An interview is an important step to securing a new opportunity. It is at the interview stage that you have the chance to reinforce your qualifications from your résumé, and position yourself as the best candidate for the role. This section provides interview tips.

Tip #98) Relax, and get ready to show your stuff.
After arriving at the interview location, and before you enter the room and meet the interviewer(s), take a deep, and be assured that you will do well, as there is nothing to panic about. Remember, if you were not qualified, you would not be at the interview, so be confident and prepared to explain why you are best suited for the position. Whether you get the job or not, be sure to give a good interview performance that you can be proud of.

Tip #99) Thank the interviewers for their consideration, and let them know you are excited to be there.

As part of introductions at the start of the interview, be sure to set the stage by thanking the interviewer(s) for inviting you and for their interest in you. Also let them know you are excited to be there and look forward to the interview. Doing this lets the interviewer(s) know that you are serious and motivated - this sets the stage for the interview being worthwhile. It also shows that you have soft skills and are personable.

Tip #100) Be conversational.

The last thing you want to be in an interview is a robot. In order to be considered for the job, you will need to give more than yes/no responses. You will be asked open-ended questions, in order for you to give particular, detailed responses. Don't be stiff, and aim to have a conversational tone. Think of it as if you were meeting someone over coffee. As such, adjust your tone, be relaxed and professional, and smile naturally - just as if you were having a conversation with someone, which actually... you are!

Tip #101) Focus on why you are best qualified for the job.

As part of your responses during the interview, ensure your responses are comprehensive and go beyond the initial questions asked. As one of your objectives is to sell yourself and make the case for why you are best qualified for the role, state your related qualities with examples, and leave a compelling case for why you should be hired.

Tip #102) Ask questions.

As part of being assessed for the job, you will be asked if you have any questions at the end of the interview. It is possible that some of your questions have been answered in the interview, and, if so, let the interviewer know that some of your questions were addressed. Saying this will let the interviewer know that, to an extent, you are both on the same page. Do not hesitate to ask questions about the job, organization, and work culture during this time. This also shows the interviewer that you are seriously considering the position.

6.0 Closing

There we have it; we have come to the end of this handbook. It is my hope that you find this resource of value as you progress through your career. Refer to it as often as needed to refresh yourself on appearance, behaviour, and communication personal image elements, and any of the related 102 tips that can affect your career.

If you have found this resource helpful, I would be delighted to hear from you! Kindly contact me at feedback@alexandergeorgegroup.com with any positive feedback or success stories. Your comments are valued and will allow me to continue refining my approaches toward continually improving my capabilities, products, and service offerings.

Best of luck to you, and in all that you do. Dream Big!

Dwayne George, PMP
BAA, MCPPM, MCBA, CBC, CMM, ICC

7.0 Log - Image Enhancement Opportunities

As your image will evolve over time, you can use the following pages to write down opportunities for your Appearance, Behaviour, and Communication enhancements. Not only will this serve as a reminder to you of Image Enhancement commitments made, but also as continued motivation as you refer back to this section over time, and see how far you have come, and what you have achieved!

7.1 Appearance Enhancement - Opportunities

Date:

Appearance Enhancement Opportunity:

Why you want to do this (your motivation):

Timeline to Achieve:

Date Goal Met:

Date:

Appearance Enhancement Opportunity:

Why you want to do this (your motivation):

Timeline to Achieve:

Date Goal Met:

PERSONAL IMAGE ENHANCEMENT - CAREER EDITION

Date:

Appearance Enhancement Opportunity:

Why you want to do this (your motivation):

Timeline to Achieve:

Date Goal Met:

Date:

Appearance Enhancement Opportunity:

Why you want to do this (your motivation):

Timeline to Achieve:

Date Goal Met:

Date:

Appearance Enhancement Opportunity:

Why you want to do this (your motivation):

Timeline to Achieve:

Date Goal Met:

Date:

Appearance Enhancement Opportunity:

Why you want to do this (your motivation):

Timeline to Achieve:

Date Goal Met:

PERSONAL IMAGE ENHANCEMENT - CAREER EDITION

Date:

Appearance Enhancement Opportunity:

Why you want to do this (your motivation):

Timeline to Achieve:

Date Goal Met:

Date:

Appearance Enhancement Opportunity:

Why you want to do this (your motivation):

Timeline to Achieve:

Date Goal Met:

Date:

Appearance Enhancement Opportunity:

Why you want to do this (your motivation):

Timeline to Achieve:

Date Goal Met:

7.2 Behaviour Enhancement - Opportunities

Date:

Behaviour Enhancement Opportunity:

Why you want to do this (your motivation):

Timeline to Achieve:

Date Goal Met:

Date:

Behaviour Enhancement Opportunity:

Why you want to do this (your motivation):

Timeline to Achieve:

Date Goal Met:

Date:

Behaviour Enhancement Opportunity:

Why you want to do this (your motivation):

Timeline to Achieve:

Date Goal Met:

Date:

Behaviour Enhancement Opportunity:

Why you want to do this (your motivation):

Timeline to Achieve:

Date Goal Met:

PERSONAL IMAGE ENHANCEMENT - CAREER EDITION

Date:

Behaviour Enhancement Opportunity:

Why you want to do this (your motivation):

Timeline to Achieve:

Date Goal Met:

Date:

Behaviour Enhancement Opportunity:

Why you want to do this (your motivation):

Timeline to Achieve:

Date Goal Met:

Date:

Behaviour Enhancement Opportunity:

Why you want to do this (your motivation):

Timeline to Achieve:

Date Goal Met:

Date:

Behaviour Enhancement Opportunity:

Why you want to do this (your motivation):

Timeline to Achieve:

Date Goal Met:

PERSONAL IMAGE ENHANCEMENT - CAREER EDITION

Date:

Behaviour Enhancement Opportunity:

Why you want to do this (your motivation):

Timeline to Achieve:

Date Goal Met:

7.3 Communication Enhancement - Opportunities

Date:

Communication Enhancement Opportunity:

Why you want to do this (your motivation):

Timeline to Achieve:

Date Goal Met:

Date:

Communication Enhancement Opportunity:

Why you want to do this (your motivation):

Timeline to Achieve:

Date Goal Met:

PERSONAL IMAGE ENHANCEMENT - CAREER EDITION

Date:

Communication Enhancement Opportunity:

Why you want to do this (your motivation):

Timeline to Achieve:

Date Goal Met:

Date:

Communication Enhancement Opportunity:

Why you want to do this (your motivation):

Timeline to Achieve:

Date Goal Met:

Date:

Communication Enhancement Opportunity:

Why you want to do this (your motivation):

Timeline to Achieve:

Date Goal Met:

Date:

Communication Enhancement Opportunity:

Why you want to do this (your motivation):

Timeline to Achieve:

Date Goal Met:

PERSONAL IMAGE ENHANCEMENT - CAREER EDITION

Date:

Communication Enhancement Opportunity:

Why you want to do this (your motivation):

Timeline to Achieve:

Date Goal Met:

Date:

Communication Enhancement Opportunity:

Why you want to do this (your motivation):

Timeline to Achieve:

Date Goal Met:

Date:

Communication Enhancement Opportunity:

Why you want to do this (your motivation):

Timeline to Achieve:

Date Goal Met:

Made in the USA
Columbia, SC
22 April 2017